What Does
the Lord Require?

D0967870

JAMES C. HOWELL

What Does the Lord Require?

Doing Justice, Loving Kindness, Walking Humbly

WJK WESTMINSTER
JOHN KNOX PRESS
LOUISVILLE · KENTUCKY

© 2012 James C. Howell
Study Guide © 2012 Westminster John Knox Press

1st edition
Published by Westminster John Knox Press
Louisville, Kentucky

12 13 14 15 16 17 18 19 20 21 — 10 9 8 7 6 5 4 3 2 1

Scripture quotations, unless otherwise indicated, are from the Revised Standard Version of the Bible, copyright © 1946, 1952, 1971, and 1973 by the Division of Christian Education of the National Council of the Churches of Christ, and are used by permission.

Book design by Drew Stevens
Cover design by Night & Day Design

Library of Congress Cataloging-in-Publication Data

Howell, James C.
    What does the Lord require? : doing justice, loving kindness,
  walking humbly / James C. Howell. -- 1st ed.
        p. cm.
    Includes bibliographical references (p.   ).
    ISBN 978-0-664-23694-6 (alk. paper)
  1. Bible. O.T. Micah VI, 8--Criticism, interpretation, etc. I. Title.
    BS1615.52.H69 2012
    224'.9306--dc23

                                    2011039964

Most Westminster John Knox Press books are available at special quantity discounts when purchased in bulk by corporations, organizations, and special-interest groups. For more information, please e-mail SpecialSales@wjkbooks.com.

CONTENTS

WHAT DOES
THE LORD REQUIRE?

O ne of the most splendid, memorable moments
in all of Scripture, and even in human history,
is the eloquent, poetic question and answer from
an obscure prophet in the late eighth century BCE.
Micah 6:8 asks, "What does the LORD require?" And
the reply is threefold: "To do justice, and to love kindness, and to walk humbly with your God." We could
spend our lives probing the beauty of these words,
with them emblazoned in our memory. More importantly, we should spend our days letting these treasured words take on reality in our lives. God would
be pleased, and we would discover the joyful reason
for our existence.

In this brief book, we will explore a few things.
Who was Micah? What was going on when he
spoke? How did his listeners receive what he

said—and how do we? Who is this God who "requires"? And what might justice, kindness, and humility look like for us?

So now we pause, give thanks to God for such provocative, lovely words, and pray for openness of mind, heart, and life so we might be transformed and satisfy our deepest desire — and God's.

1

MICAH THE PROPHET

We wish we knew more about Micah as a person. His parents must have been full of faith and gratitude when he was born, for they named him Micah, which in Hebrew is an exclamation, a rhetorical question, a burst of praise meaning, "Who is like the Lord?" Who indeed! God is incomparable. We may say God is like the best parent ever, or a benevolent king, or the sun rising; but the name Micah rolls all those up into one and declares that God is exponentially more wonderful than them all. We never figure God out or box God in; we might pray for long life so we can continue in our quest to learn more and more about this God who is mind-bogglingly more fantastic than the sharpest mind or the most passionate heart could ever understand. Who is like the Lord?

This name, Micah, has been one of the most

popular names in all of human history, in countless cultures and languages, morphing into kindred forms like Micaiah, Michael, Mike, and Miguel. Hans Walter Wolff has suggested that "it may be the oldest name that has survived more than 4,000 years and remained undiminished in popularity down to the present time."[1]

Such a name is a badge of honor, and an inescapable challenge: Could Micah's life be a humble reply to the rhetorical question "Who is like the Lord?" He hailed from a small village called Moreshet, located about twenty miles southwest of Jerusalem. Micah's family dealt with catastrophe and immense sorrow: Moreshet was one of forty-six towns destroyed by the Assyrian emperor Sennacherib when he invaded Judah, bent on world domination. Micah and his family were forced to flee to Jerusalem for safety, looking over their shoulders to see their hometown being burned and reduced to rubble. How did Micah feel when he arrived in what was supposed to be the Holy City, Mount Zion—for it was the political leadership in Jerusalem whose foolish foreign policy and failure of faith had brought the Assyrian juggernaut down on villages like Moreshet!

Micah, more in sync with God's vision than those who were supposed to be the holy leaders in the capital city, became a critic of the government bureaucracy and of the vapid spiritual leadership. An idea like the separation of church and state would have struck Israel as absurd, and Micah spoke a strong word from the incomparable Lord against those who made a travesty of politics and religion. His harshest prophecy? "Zion shall be plowed as a field; Jerusalem shall become a heap of ruins" (Mic. 3:12). City officials must have been mortified, or perhaps they chuckled at this country bumpkin talking about a plow in a stone-paved city. They fantasized that the Lord would come to rescue them, but Micah turned their hope on its ear: "For behold, the LORD is coming. . . . And the mountains will melt. . . . All this is for the transgression of Jacob and for the sins of the house of Israel" (1:3–5). The prophet exposed the leaders who pretended to be good but were greedy and crushed the poor. And he was vindicated: Jerusalem *did* become a heap of ruins.

Micah was bold in denunciation, but he was even bolder in hope. The fifth chapter of Micah, with its yearning that a messiah would be born in another little hick town, Bethlehem, is read in churches during Advent and Christmas; and his vision of that glorious day when swords will be beaten into plowshares and spears into pruning hooks (4:3) is a dream that echoes through the ages.

In this book, we will reflect on another beautiful, compelling thought Micah shared directly from the mind and heart of God. He would not accept an award for being a brilliant author or an accomplished religious thinker; he heard God say something (and we wish we knew how he heard God!); and like a messenger, he repeated it. "'With what shall I come before the LORD? . . . He has showed you, . . . what is good; and what does the

LORD require of you but to do justice, and to love kindness, and to walk humbly with your God?'" (6:6–8). Micah, whose name was a question, asks a question. When did he first say these words? Surely he repeated them on another day, perhaps quite a few times. Who was standing around to listen? What was their reaction? What did his voice sound like? What did his face, his eyes, look like? Did he gesture? Who thought to write it down? Can we sense the urgency, the severity, the tenderness in these words?

2

A CONTROVERSY

We do not know where in Jerusalem Micah first revealed God's urgent question. But since Micah uses the technical language of a trial (or in Hebrew, a *rîb*), he could have heightened the drama by speaking near the city's entrance. In ancient times, the courtroom was out of doors; cases were settled in the stone corridors that led into the city, out in the sun and dust. With smooth rocks for furniture, the wise elders of the village wrinkled their brows, listened, weighed the evidence, and decided the case.

For Micah's imaginative trial, a small crowd might have assembled by the gate, and very quickly they would have understood that Micah was creating something of a court scene—and that they were the defendants being put on trial! "Arise, plead your case. . . . The LORD has a controversy with his people, and he will contend with Israel" (Mic. 6:1–2). Much has happened between God and these people; conflict has flared, and nothing is left to do but to determine innocence and guilt — and more importantly, to sift through the evidence and come to some sort of resolution to the conflict.

We may prefer not to think of our relationship with God as conflictual. But the whole premise of sin, our very need for grace, is this: God does not leave our waywardness unaddressed. Micah asks his listeners to imagine a court case in which God presents pointed charges against the people; the gravity of their offense is underlined because God also produces a mountain of evidence of God's stunning goodness to them in the face of their apathy and lunacy. This idea of a trial might strike us as legalistic, but due legal process affirms the dignity of everyone involved. God cannot permit anarchy, yet frontier justice or a backwoods lynching won't do either. If God were a lesser sort of divinity, God could simply squash us or cast us into oblivion. But in a trial, judge and jury, accused and accuser, must all listen, weigh, consider, converse, and decide. It's the glory of humanity (and of God!) that God treats us with respect.

God is the injured party. And sitting behind the defendant's table, looking a bit sheepish, wishing the clock could be rewound, trying to figure out how to get out of this mess, is — well — it's Israel, but it's also us. We are the ones the Lord is accusing. And the Lord is looking for justice, for some redress. Our pockets aren't nearly deep enough for the fine we suspect we'll owe, and jail time would almost be a relief. Didn't this Lord say something about setting prisoners free?

The witnesses sworn in to testify are impeccable. God calls on creation itself—mountains, the foundations of the earth—to speak. God's goodness, and our good cause to trust in this God, are as old as Methuselah, more ancient than the Stone Age or dinosaurs or the first moment billions of years ago when God hurled the universe into being. Our dependence upon God, our accountability to God, our hope in God are woven into the very fabric of the world, more solid than the ground we stand on, more vital than the air we breathe.

History is another witness in this trial. God, with a touch of irony, asks the people, "What have I done to you?" Done *to* you? Done *for* you! God chidingly reminds the people of the great acts of God: delivering the people from bondage, patiently rescuing them over and over from danger, loving them, mercifully sticking with them literally for centuries. What counterargument would a defendant mount against such an open-and-shut case?

The people who first heard Micah probably responded the way we do today: a bit defensive at first, then with a shrinking sensation. Oh, why, why, why have we been so stupid? The Israelites who first heard Micah's words worshiped at the magnificent temple of Solomon in Jerusalem. In Israel's worship, you never approached God empty-handed. You brought a lamb, a heifer, at least a turtledove or some grain. But now the people can only shrug, their spiritual pockets empty; they have nothing to bring before the Lord but their failure, their guilt, their obtuse waywardness.

Perhaps when they heard Micah, they recalled a dramatic moment from the last time they had worshiped. They had said all the right words, been through the motions, and had even believed themselves to be fairly honest and even faithful in their worship. The throng would cluster outside the gate of the temple, and then the priest would come out to invite the community into the holy precincts. But first, a few questions:

> O Lord, who shall sojourn in thy tent?
> Who shall dwell on thy holy hill?
> —Ps. 15:1

> Who shall ascend the hill of the Lord?
> And who shall stand in his holy place?
> —Ps. 24:3

They had themselves uttered the traditional replies:

> He who has clean hands and a pure heart,
> who does not lift up his soul to what is false,
> and does not swear deceitfully
> —Ps. 24:4

> He who . . . speaks truth from his heart;
> who does not slander with his tongue,
> and does no evil to his friend,

nor takes up a reproach against his neighbors;

. . . .

who does not put out his money at interest,
and does not take a bribe against the innocent.

—Ps. 15:2–5

Perhaps now they realized their hypocrisy, their faked religiosity, their intense guilt. They expected Micah to rub it in, to give them a moral thrashing.

Perhaps we can imagine ourselves, standing with them, bracing for Micah's denunciation. But then unexpectedly, the curtains begin to rustle a bit, a shutter flies open, and a breeze bolts into the room, across the plaza, cooling their cheeks. Heads turn—and the judge announces the verdict. Guilty, of course, as expected. But the sentence? What will be required of us who have exhibited a flimsy faith, a failure of nerve, a gross inability to pay much attention to the things of God?

3

GOD HAS SHOWN YOU WHAT IS GOOD

So what will God require? Surprisingly, and tenderly, God pauses just a moment, refusing to declare a harsh sentence. Just before God announces what will be required of the guilty, Micah adds a merciful reminder: "He has shown you what is good." It is hard to imagine a more hopeful sentence. It is impossible to overstate the glory of this truth. God could leave us guessing; God could be capricious and throw us off balance; God could have set little traps for us or hidden the will of God under huge boulders or in the depths of the ocean. But no: "He has shown you what is good."

In fact, the whole witness of the Bible is precisely this: God has shown us what is good. The story of creation, the chronicle of blessing, the call of Abraham, the deliverance of Israel from bondage in

Egypt, the revealing gift of God's law on Mt. Sinai, the provision of land, a temple, a way to reconcile with God and others through sacrifice and forgiveness, the wisdom of sages, the marvel of worship: God has shown you what is good.

In Genesis, God made the world, and called it—and us!—good, charging us to take care of the place. God called Abraham—and us!—to be a blessing to everybody else. God used scoundrels like Jacob—and us!—to further the divine plan. God commanded the people—and us!—to be holy. God spoke to Israel—and to us!—through the prophets. God's signature was scribbled on the good earth, on the Scriptures, on the ways of worship, on the very plot of history. For Christians, God sent Jesus, God's own Son, to teach, to heal, to reconcile, to love, to die and be raised from the dead. God's Spirit has vivified the church and raised up saints and teachers and sanctuaries that inspire us. What more could we ask for? God has shown us in manifold ways what is good.

Notice that Micah doesn't say God has shown you what is good, but you blew it, you missed out, and now you are toast. The invitation remains open; God's patience cannot be ruffled. God has not left us to our own devices. Sometimes we may feel puzzled or downright buffaloed about God's will: What does God want? Maybe in heaven God will answer all our questions! But God wants us to know what God wants more than we want to know what God wants—and now, not in the hazy future. God is literally dying to show us what is good; we believe this was Jesus' saving mission. Certainly to know and live for God is challenging; we have to dig in, probe, reflect, mess up, and try again—which is the beauty of it. But God has told us what we need to know: "God has made known to us the mystery of his will" (Eph. 1:9).

And while Micah doesn't delve into it, God has shown us what is good—but with a twist. There remains a hidden dimension to this revelation of what God requires. St. Augustine once prayed at length to God about his life, acknowledging his inability to get done what he knew God wanted him to get done. What was his most profound plea to God? "My entire hope is exclusively in your very great mercy. Grant what you command, and command what you will."[1] How God provides in us and through us what God requires remains to be seen. For now, since God has shown us what is good, let us see what then is required.

4

WHAT THE LORD REQUIRES

The whole idea of what God "requires" casts God in the image of a high school algebra teacher, collecting worksheets, grading quizzes, alternating between the dreaded red X marks and the more welcome checkmarks. Am I going to pass? Is there a curve?

Micah 6:8 isn't a final exam. What God "requires" is far more personal, intimate, and marvelous than a menu of items to adhere to or not. Micah is about to tell us what God "requires," and to understand, we need to shift our mind-set from the algebra quiz to living things. A child requires the tenderness of his mother. A flower requires sunshine and rain. My body requires oxygen, the dolphin requires water, the wise old sage requires a visit from his adoring student. There is a mutuality in this holy kind of requiring. Yes, God requires a certain kind of life from us, but the life flows two ways. A child requires affection from his mother, but the mother quite effortlessly gives it — and needs it herself from the child. The oxygen and rain are there for people and flowers; they are simply givens, gifts, all grace. We really can pray, "Grant what you command, and command what you will."

The Hebrew word Micah used (or God used through Micah!) that we translate "require" is fascinating, complex, and far more lovely than the rigidity implied by "require." A brief Hebrew lesson might help us: We find *darař* in various situations, not many of which feel like class with the algebra teacher. Rebekah is pregnant with twins, and they are struggling so fiercely in her womb that she *darař*es God for help or understanding; when King David spies the lovely Bathsheba bathing, he *darař*es — that is, he tries to learn more about who she is (2 Sam. 11:3). Lovers *darař* one another, meaning simply that they care deeply (Jer. 30:14); a shepherd *darař*es an animal that has strayed (Deut. 22:2). There is a seeking, a refusal to settle for distance, at the heart of this verb *darař*. Isaiah, speaking during the days of Micah, declares that God's people should *darař* "justice" (which Micah is about to say God *darař*es!); they should seek it, be intent upon it, not settle for a lack of justice.

So the people *darař* justice, and God *darař*es justice! We see the mutuality in *darař*ing inherent in the word. When the people worship, they *darař* the Lord: they seek, they try to connect to God, they establish a channel of blessing. When troubled politicians need to know a word from the Lord, they ask (*darař*) for it. The scribe Ezra unfurls the scroll of God's law and studies diligently; he *daraĭes* the Scripture. How marvelous: When Micah ruminates with the people over what God "requires," he uses the word they use for what they do when they try to find God, to hear from God, which is the same word they use for the way a man feels for his beloved. What God is feeling through Micah's words, and what God seeks in mutuality with the people, is something intensely personal, reciprocal. God is not striving to pour religious facts into our heads or to elicit flat behaviors. Anything that is *daraĭed* is personal; it matters. We are probing deep into the heart, and the distance between the seeker and the one sought is narrowed. The care, the curiosity, the power flow two ways. What God craves matches precisely our deepest desire: *daraĭ* embraces *daraĭ*.

We obviously are a long way from a high-control God who "requires" as in "insists." Some people see God as an omnipotent manipulator of events; to them, everything that happens is God's will. Why even speak of what God "requires," since all that happens is already willed by God? But this is wrong; God doesn't coerce: "Love does not insist on its own way" (1 Cor. 13:5). God loves, God *daraĭes*, God seeks, God gives us space to *daraĭ* God right back. This is God's ultimate show of power: it is the power to love, to risk, to leave us space to respond. All God's doing throughout Scripture exhibits this God, who isn't an enforcer of rules but who has a heart overflowing with passion.

We can only understand what God "requires" in light of what God has done, and God has been creative, imaginative, flexible, even lavish! Consider

God's infinite love for creation, for the fields and birds, for Jacob, Sarah, David, Micah himself, and his listeners; consider that Jesus criticized harshly the self-righteous who firmly believed they had done all that God required. Yet he embraced people who had never thought twice about the requirements of Micah 6:8, and he sought them the way a shepherd seeks a lost lamb. Jesus asked for their love, their loyalty, their *daraśing*, waving his hand as he headed down the road and said, "Follow me."

"What God requires" is really an engraved invitation: God—the good God who made you, who gives you air, life, love, and purpose—this God requires your presence! How could your response be anything but a breathless urgency? I've received an invitation to dinner by the richest person on earth, the king of a great domain, the rock star I've fawned over all my life. Do I just toss it? Or do I lay it on my desk while I think about it? *No*, I answer, and now, with a chiseled-in-stone commitment: *Yes, yes, of course. Yes I will come! God requires my presence, my life, my all? Yes.* What other answer could there be?

Sadly there is another answer. We delay, our attention drifts, the weeds of sin thrive. We don't follow, we get haywire and out of sync with God. This is the paradox: God gives what God requires, but we still falter. Not only do we fail; we realize we don't have enough stashed in our attics or bank accounts to make a dent in what would be sufficient for God; we lack confidence to realize God's gift of what God requires. Sarah McLachlan wrote a simple yet profound lyric in her song "Fear": "I fear

I have nothing to give, and I have so much to lose here in this lonely place."

The verses that lead up to Micah 6:8 ask with zealous passion (but humble awareness that we can't do nearly enough), "With what shall I come before the LORD?" Burnt offerings? Calves? Thousands of rams? Tens of thousands of rivers of oil? Notice the crescendo of the inquiry. *Is this enough? I sense not. Is this enough? Still not enough? How about this?* The heightening of possible offerings to God borders on the absurd: What if I could offer what I don't even have? What if I could offer what only the richest person on earth could offer?

For Micah's listeners, the question is tragically funny: They have nothing to offer anyhow. The economy is in shambles, and the Assyrian army is camped on the hillside, with the sun glistening off their bronze and iron shields, swords, and armor. You couldn't lay your hands on a calf or ram if you wanted to offer it to God. But what if we could? Would it ever be enough? Is God really a God who needs to be placated? Is the God who has shown us what is good the type of deity who virtually becomes an enemy we must buy off with religious acts?

Or what if I even made the ultimate sacrifice: "Shall I give my first-born for my transgression?" (Mic. 6:7). We have crossed a significant barrier, haven't we? Instead of merely offering God things, even a grand host of things I have never possessed, what does it mean when the heart reaches deeper to consider offering God what is more precious than life itself—the one I love?

Echoes of the harrowing, unforgettable story of Abraham and Isaac haunt us. Abraham and Sarah waited forever, beyond human possibility, for the child who finally was born. How much is the impossible child loved, the one wanted for so very long? We may feel confused by God's requirement that Abraham kill this beloved child, but could it be that God really requires not one but two things? God requires Abraham to put his total trust, his very heart, his future and whatever meaning it might hold, into God's hands. And God requires not the death but the *life* of this child!

This dual requirement is a clue into what God requires through the prophet Micah. God does love sacrifice, when we give things that are precious to God and when we obey God's laws. But what was Jesus after in the Sermon on the Mount? He was mildly interested in the avoidance of acts of murder and adultery, but he cut to the heart and was on a mission to free our souls from anger and lust (Matt. 5:21–28). The sacrifice of a ram is mildly interesting to God, but it is the heart God covets. In a way, the words of Micah feel like God fuming over our failure, but as John Calvin suggested when he preached on Micah 6, "Whenever God chides his people, he opens to them the door of hope."[1]

"What does God require?" is the wrong question, we now see. Instead, we are led to ask, "Whom does God require?" And the answer would be . . . "Me, and you—all of us." God doesn't require any *thing*; nothing external to ourselves will do. God requires us, ourselves, our lives, hearts, passion, zeal, devotion, time, thoughts, and love; God has given us things, but

God's real gift is God's own self. At the same time, God requires not the death of us but our life. God gives life—in the very requirements that seem to be hard, sacrificial, costly. What a relief that we don't have enough. What a relief that we even need mercy so desperately, for that means we receive mercy! Yet at the very point of receiving mind-boggling, unachievable mercy, our striving to do things for God and to offer up our very selves to God intensifies; we are then unbound and set free.

You don't have to be somebody you aren't. God requires you to be yourself—your truest self, the one God made you to be, the one trapped in the shell of your phony self, struggling to get out. You don't have to be Mother Teresa or St. Francis, but you also don't have to be your old self, frustrated by doing little for God.

The dawning of God's reign is not up to us; we cannot make it happen. But we can prepare the way. Our repentance, our faithfulness, our determination to be the people God made us to be is the prelude, the overture to the great symphony of what God surely will do—because God promised. God makes and keeps all promises. God requires, and God will give what God requires.

And when we open ourselves to what God requires, God is "pleased" (Mic. 6:7); God takes delight in us. We can do this to the heart of God? We know we can break God's heart, but we can also please God and bring great joy to God, who never stops *daraš*ing us and wants nothing more or less than that we *daraš* God in the mutuality of love.

5

THREE THINGS

The Lord has shown us what is good—and the good that we are shown by God is precisely what God requires, what God gives, what pleases God, what delights us. On the edge of our seats now, we can't wait any longer. What is it God requires? We expect it to be one thing—or perhaps a million things. Probably it's not a million, since Micah 6 already admits that burnt offerings, calves, thousands of rams, and ten thousand rivers of oil won't do. *One*, though, is a frequent Bible answer. To the rich young ruler, Jesus says, "One thing you lack" (Luke 18:22); to Martha, Jesus says, "One thing is necessary" (Luke 10:42); the psalmist sang, "One thing have I asked of the LORD" (Ps. 27:4).

But in Micah 6:8, the number is three: "To do justice, and to love kindness, and to walk humbly with your God." But this isn't a checklist: Justice? Got it. Kindness? Working on it. Walk humbly? Maybe someday. The lines between the three are blurry. Justice requires humility, which induces kindness, which looks a lot like humility, as does real justice. Justice is a different kind of justice because it is paired with walking humbly, and kindness has a different edge since it is situated between justice and walking humbly. Micah's intent for us cannot be that lyric from the pop song, "Two out of three ain't bad." We need all three, which are really one, or we miss all three—and God. Perhaps the same way a tripod can't hold a camera without all three legs functioning, perhaps the way southern iced tea just isn't right without the tea, the lemon, and the sugar, we cannot see God without doing justice, and loving kindness, and walking humbly. It is the "threefold cord" that "is not quickly broken" (Eccl. 4:12).

The three are one—the way one might try to describe a wonderful piece of sculpture by standing in the front, then moving to the side to glimpse a fresh perspective, then around the back for yet more insight. The three are one—the way you can't quite sum up your whole life in a single adjective, but you acknowledge a mix of optimistic, sad, and weary, or fun-loving, anxious, and lonely, or serious, content, and hopeful. The three are one— the way God can't be known to us simply as one, although we know God is one. God is three: Father, Son, Holy Spirit, Jesus standing in the Jordan River, the Father's voice from above, the Spirit-dove swooping down.

We like the pattern "three" evokes in our mind. How many jokes begin, "Three guys went to . . ." or "There was a priest, a rabbi, and an imam . . ."? It could be that we have heard this threeness so often it is imprinted in our brain, and hence is appealing. Yet it might also be that if God is in fact three—Father, Son, and Holy Spirit—then there are "vestiges" of the Trinity all through life and creation itself. Over the centuries, our wisest theologians have relished these vestiges they have detected. Could it be that Micah 6:8 is another vestige, a prophetic echo, of the inner life of God? Micah never heard of the Trinity and might have been prepared to duke it out with you if you dared to suggest God isn't merely "one." But the one thing this one God requires happens to be three: "to do justice, and to love kindness, and to walk humbly with your God."

The "with God" is crucial, and life-giving, as we will see. These are not three isolated notions that stand on their own as stellar ideas. They are all from the heart of God and intensely personal. If you don't know this God, these three might not make much sense, or our understanding of them will be skewed. And these are not timeless notions; they are timely, they fit this moment, just as they fit Micah's Iron Age moment. Don't humility, kindness, and justice shift in tone throughout your own life? God requires humility now, but like it or not, as we move toward the end of our lives, we all wind up humbled. Often, kindness grows later in life, as the hardness molts away and we finally, later than we wish, become tender, and a peculiar kind of justice is rendered.

Since the three are one—and if you untangled a threefold cord you couldn't be sure which was the first in the rope maker's hand, and a tripod would fail without one of its legs—I have wondered in what order to consider justice, kindness, and walking humbly. Justice will not make sense without kindness, and walking humbly is a prerequisite for anything good in our life with God. But let us follow Micah's order, or that of the God who inspired him to speak, but with a readiness to drift among the three to be sure we are sensing the heart of God.

6

TO DO JUSTICE

God has shown us what God "requires," *daraves*, seeks, provides, and shares with us, and in our triad the first (not in importance, but simply the first Micah mentions) is this: "to do justice." It seems that God does not merely want us to *want* justice, or to *wish* justice would happen; God seems uninterested in any whining we might do because of a lack of justice. God does not say, "Think about justice," or "Campaign for justice," or even "Pray for justice," although these may be superb, holy activities pleasing to God.

For now, God simply yearns for us to do justice. Justice is something we *do*; it is an action, involving energy and effort, a habit across time, not an occasional burst or something applied only in a crisis. Doing can be seen; justice apparently happens only if we get moving, and sweat a little. A life of faith that is delightful to God has some muscle to it, and onlookers can see something is really happening. God *daraʃes* justice that is tangible.

Micah does not say, "Enforce justice." We have law enforcement that ensures a kind of justice and that battles the dark side of justice's failure; the Bible knows and advocates this kind of justice. Victims of evil are lifted up when perpetrators are apprehended, and the community cannot thrive if crime and injustice are not addressed firmly.

But God isn't speaking merely to judges, lawyers, and policemen when God says, "Do justice." Every person, young and old, tall and short, healthy or sick, brilliant or slow—and not only each individual, but all the individuals together, the whole community as a community, all the clans and tribes together as a nation are called to "Do justice."

To do justice, we need to know what it is we are supposed to do. What is justice? The Hebrew word *mishpat* can mean simply a law, an ordinance. In Exodus, a *mishpat* is a specific commandment from God; the plural, *mishpatim*, are the legal teachings God passed down through Moses to the people so they might possess the land and have life. So justice is what God has established as the very specific ways people are to act. When Micah says, "Do justice," he means, "Do these commandments; do the things God told us to do on Mt. Sinai!"

Christians, who bask in the wonder of grace, recoil a bit in the face of a commanding God. We like to think of God not as a judge issuing laws and keeping account of how we are doing, but as a gracious, benevolent, kindly sort of deity who is merciful and loves us no matter what. We may even pity the Israelites, for surely they chafed under the burden of so many picayune commandments from their Lord! But the Israelites, at least on their more faithful days, were grateful for the law. What would life be like if God had refrained from creating a world with some rights and wrongs, and if God had not "shown us what is good"?

In Psalm 19 we overhear a robust appreciation for God's commandments:

> The law of the LORD is perfect,
>   reviving the soul;
>
> .   .   .   .
>
> the precepts of the LORD are right,
>   rejoicing the heart;
> the commandment of the LORD is pure,
>   enlightening the eyes;
>
> .   .   .   .
>
> the ordinances of the LORD are true,
>   and righteous altogether.
> More to be desired are they than gold,
>   even much fine gold;
> sweeter also than honey,
>   and drippings of the honeycomb.
>
> .   .   .   .
>
> In keeping them there is great reward.
>   —Ps. 19:7–11

The law graciously mapped out the way to the joy and freedom of inner purity, gave wise counsel on how to farm or raise animals in ways that were in sync with the Creator's wiring of the universe, and provided a means of reconciliation when relationships were fractured. Doing these *mishpatim* made one smarter, nobler, happier. God got into Micah's vocal cords and reminded the people, "Do justice," for it was precisely the Israelites' persistent fudging on these matters, bending them to their own advantage or simply pretending God had never spoken that got them into trouble.

But Micah 6:8's understanding of justice is far more than, and actually quite a bit different from, simple rules for the smooth ordering of society, to protect us from crime or to access benefits. These commandments, these *mishpatim*, are not good ideas that could work anywhere with any people who believed anything. There were plenty of law codes in ancient times, Hammurabi's being the most famous. But in Israel, justice is personal, personal *to* God and personal as in *from* God. Justice reveals what is in the heart of God. God's people, precisely because they are God's, are charged with enacting the justice that is really God's. Since justice is God's, how precious is it? People would go to great lengths to hear it and to receive it. Deborah sat under a palm tree, where the people came to her for *mishpat* (Judg. 4:5). So highly valued was this *mishpat* that when people came to Absalom for it, he was able to "steal their hearts" (2 Sam. 15:2–6).

The failure to deliver *mishpat* was especially despicable; Samuel's sons "did not walk in his ways, but turned aside after gain; they took bribes and perverted justice [*mishpat*]" (1 Sam. 8:3).

In fact, *mishpat* has everything to do with restraint on this issue of "gain," and with stealing hearts. The more we explore the word, the more we notice a steady chorus of texts that say judgment, *mishpat*, cannot be deferential to the rich. There is a special bias in *mishpat* toward the poor, and even to the outsider, the sojourner, or the foreigner, who in most societies in those days would have been despised and had no protection at all (Lev. 19:15; 24:22). It is repeatedly emphasized that when *mishpat* dawns, small and great alike are heard. Bribes, slick attorneys, and political leverage are anathema to *mishpat*. Bias toward the haves is upended; the have-nots may have nothing else, but they will have *mishpat*. God's *mishpat* inspires and settles for no less than a radical leveling, and the uncomfortable de-privileging of those who are canny enough to get ahead. Such an arrangement isn't a liberal quest for fairness or equality; rather, this style of justice simply mirrors the heart and mind of God, and keeping this holy *mishpat* gives life to the people (Deut. 4:1; 6:20).

We need not be surprised at this peculiar brand of justice, since it flows from the heart of God. God has a powerful inclination toward lifting up the have-nots. While Israel is encouraged to do well by the have-nots, the Israelites also realize that in reality they *are* the have-nots, they are the ones in need of not merely a kind of mercy but a truer sort of justice, in which God refuses special privilege to the powerful and empowers the lowly.

Mishpat is God's dream for a special kind of community. In fact, the goal of justice, the goal of all those laws God gave Moses on Mt. Sinai, all those *mishpatim* together, was a community, the ongoing relationships of tribes, clans, kin—but also strangers. Justice raises the question: What kind of people are we going to be? Since Israel's God is a bit of an oddball compared to the divinities of other ancient cultures, we might expect this God's justice to be a bit strange—and therefore wonderful and life-giving. Israel's God is the defender of the poor and oppressed (Jer. 9:23; Ps. 10:17; Isa. 59:15–16). "[God] executes justice for the fatherless and the widow" (Deut. 10:18), who have no other legal counsel, no backing, no one to stand beside them.

If Israelite society was to mirror the heart of such a God, then Israel was required to provide justice for the orphan, the poor, the disadvantaged, the stranger. In fact, a thumbnail summary of what *mishpat* justice is about in Israel would be this: *justice is when the poorest are cared for*. A just society is not necessarily the one where fairness reigns and the diligent and thrifty are rewarded. No, a just society is the one where everyone belongs, where the neediest are taken good care of, where no one is hungry or disenfranchised.

Walter Brueggemann suggests that justice requires us "to sort out what belongs to whom, and to return it to them."[1] Implied in his definition is that all Israel has—the land, the produce, the sunshine and rain, the breath of life and other people with whom to share it—belongs not to the individual who might have a name on a deed, but to God! When Israel came into the land of Canaan, God divided up the land so everyone would have some land, so everyone would have enough. If one farm failed, the prosperous farmer couldn't just gobble it up; the land was owned in perpetuity by all the families, so the whole capitalist enterprise of haves and have-nots was undermined.

In Haiti, there is a proverb: "God gives, but God doesn't share." God has given us plenty, enough for everybody; but the sharing is up to us. The ancient Israelites would call this radical sharing "justice," *mishpat*. In modern times, sometimes we use different terminology, like "the rights of the disadvantaged" or "social entitlements"; but the tone of these ideas is more hostile, individualistic, destructive of community. The idea of "rights," so vaunted in Western democracies, can become shrill and demanding—and isolating: "I shall have my rights!" But in ancient Israel, you do not have a "right" to life, for life is a *gift* of God; you do not have a right to a wage or basic necessities, since God has graciously created us as part of a community where sharing and support are as natural as what a parent does for a toddler.

And certainly in Israel, food or care or shelter would never be conceived as an "entitlement." The titles all belong to God; the land is God's, the rain comes down from God's hand, the sunshine and fruit and breath and all that is good are sheer grace, belonging to God but mercifully bestowed on beloved people who crave nothing but the pleasure of God. And God's pleasure, when it comes to the disbursement of God's good, is *mishpat*.

The justice Micah 6:8 invites us to do is *mishpat*, sharing what God has given, enacting God's will not merely for oneself but for the people, and with a zealous determination to ensure that not one person is left out in the cold, that no child ever dies from hunger, that even the most difficult, strange, hard-to-love person is loved and included. A statue outside the Supreme Court in Washington, D.C., depicts justice as a blindfolded woman holding up a balanced scale. Justice is blind—and in a way, *mishpat* is blind. No special regard is given to status or background; emotion, allegiance, and passion are to be removed from the equation. God's justice is unswayed by status or the possibility of corrupt profit. But God is far from blind. With eyes wide open, God looks at each person and is far from neutral or impassive. God loves, God's emotion reigns, God's compassion trumps in every time. Love and affection are not inimical to justice but are at the very heart of what God is after with the creatures God made and continues to cherish in God's heart.

But justice, for God, never settles for being a mere idea or emotion; God wants *mishpat* to happen. The Lord "requires" that we do justice. How practical and thus how real—and how challenging. Here is a *mishpat* God gave Moses on Mt. Sinai:

"When you reap the harvest of your land, you shall not reap your field to its very border; . . . you shall not strip your vineyard bare, neither shall you gather the fallen grapes of your vineyard; you shall leave them for the poor and for the sojourner: I am the LORD your God" (Lev. 19:9–10). The crop has finally matured, my family is hungry, the year has proven to be lean, I am exhausted but excited—but I can't reap it all for myself? To leave the grapes I accidentally dropped, to leave desperately needed grain ungathered, is a physically embodied reenactment of what we can only call grace, a tangible echo of the love in God's heart for me, and for others who have not earned what they are now receiving—not from my gracious hand, but God's. What more powerful visual illustration could there be of justice (or of God's grace) than this? Who gets the grain and grapes? Anybody who is hungry. God's goodness is not to be hoarded, but spread around, made available for free to strangers. The average Israelite had to *do* something so as not to squander the covenant, or the Israelites together had to engage in certain practices so as not to jar the lovely order of the cosmos established in grace by the Lord.

All Christians, if they look back in time, will discern that doing *mishpat* is in their charter. As a United Methodist, I treasure John Wesley's counsel "to carry relief to the poor, not just to send it," to visit debtors in prison, to take in orphans, and to redistribute what little wealth there might have been.[2] We do not merely receive grace; we must put it to work. And when grace is put to work, when *mishpat* begins to happen, onlookers notice, and evangelism stands a chance of success. How else will we persuade modern-day cynics to take an interest in the life of faith if we do not care radically for the neediest?

This kind of *mishpat* can't be a one-off, a little spasm of *mishpat* when it is convenient. Micah 6:8 asks us to do justice, not merely at Thanksgiving or Christmas when we blithely think it is part of the spirit of the season to give away an old coat or send a toy to some pitiable child. Justice is a habit, a discipline, all year long, in all of life. Amos, who was a neighbor and slightly older contemporary of Micah (did they know each other?), spoke for God: "But let justice roll down like waters, and righteousness like an everflowing stream" (Amos 5:24).

God requires justice constantly, the way lovers require one another, the way Ezra probed the Scriptures, the way families rally around one who is struggling.

Justice is not mere charity, although it involves charity. Justice not only gives to the poor; *mishpat* asks why poverty exists and whether there are systems and structures that create poverty or that grind people into the pavement instead of lifting them up. Justice will involve advocacy, as we become the voice of those who have no voice.

Justice doesn't merely do good for somebody at a distance. Charles Dickens spoke of "telescopic philanthropy,"[3] the sort of sentiment that delights in having aid sent to someone at a far, convenient distance. Justice gets up close; mishpat delivers aid and befriends the one in need. Justice inevitably involves reconciliation.

Thinking back to that verb *darasɪ*, which we often translate "require": What does the Lord require? To do justice. The root *darasɪ* winds up in the noun *midrash*. We could fill a large library with countless volumes of Jewish midrash! A midrash is an interpretation, a paraphrase, an application of the text in a new situation, drawing out its deeper meaning and reading between the lines to discern how Scripture fits right now, and here. The rabbis believed all the secrets of the universe were tucked away in Scripture, and it was the responsibility of midrash to deduce those from the text and apply eternal truths to human experience. To do justice, we must connect this ancient concept with real people with real needs. We must listen and find the peculiar application of justice here and now, not then and there.

To do justice, no petrified method will do. We cannot treat every person identically. All are equal in God's eyes, but God made each person in a unique way, with a never-to-be-repeated matrix of feelings, perceptions, strengths, foibles, backgrounds, abilities, and passions; each wound each person suffers is unique, so to repair each hurt requires a midrash of sorts, an interpretation, a discovery of fresh meaning for the event or the person at hand. Every person is our neighbor (Luke 10:25–37), but no two neighbors are alike. So we must look at each one; we must be steady listeners and creative in our application of what *mishpat* will look like for this person. We do not ask, "What do I want to do for this person in need?" Rather, we ask, "What does this person in need really need? What will really help—not me to feel good about helping, but the actual person who is no longer the target of my doing good, but a friend?

Is there a limit on how far *mishpat* can go? Certainly we will never get justice fully spread around as we might wish, but the idea of any boundary is appalling. Someone got the brilliant idea that churches should pray, "Lord, send us the people that nobody else wants." What congregation could be immune from praying this prayer, or eagerly welcoming and even seeking out (*darashing!*) the unwanted?

Who gets *mishpat*? Jesus said, "Love your enemies" (Matt. 5:44) and give your cloak to the one who has wrongfully taken your coat (Matt. 5:40). Justice isn't the punishment of enemies; *mishpat* is caring for them. In our world, it could well be that the reason we have so much war and violence is precisely because justice has failed, and we will never have peace until we learn how to lift up the enemy and do justice. And we do justice whether it appears to be working or not, and we persist. People of hope do not calculate probabilities of success; we do *mishpat* because it is just, it is in the heart of God, it is what we were made for. James, the brother of our Lord, said that this is true religion: "to visit orphans and widows in their affliction," to be "doers of the word, and not hearers only" (Jas. 1:27, 22).

Finally, we cannot limit the doing of *mishpat* merely to this or that individual. Our midrash of justice will lead us to broken communities: a slum, a neighborhood slammed by a plant closing, a city whose economy is in the doldrums. We zero in on societies and cultures and seek *mishpat* everywhere, in every way. This is what the Lord requires.

7

TO LOVE KINDNESS

Micah's first requirement, *mishpat*, is easy to translate as "justice," but we do find ourselves reoriented with a fresh, deeper understanding of what it really involves. When we consider Micah's second requirement, though, his words from 2,700 years ago are nearly impossible to translate—although if we are diligent, we can understand what he had in mind and can even begin to live up to this requirement that may be the linchpin of God's threefold yearning for our life with God.

We can compare translations. The 1611 King James Version made Western civilization familiar with "to love mercy" (followed in this by the New International Version). The 1948 Revised Standard Version updated that a bit "to love kindness" (echoed exactly by the New Revised Standard

Version and the New American Standard Bible). The Jerusalem Bible chose "to love loyalty," the Jewish Publication Society "to love goodness," the Good News Bible "to show constant love," and Eugene Peterson's paraphrase, *The Message*, tried "to be compassionate and loyal in your love."

All these together touch on some aspect or another of what Micah was trying to say, but not one of them captures the rich depth of the terms involved. The Hebrew is short and crisp: *ahavat ḥesed* — just two words! The first word, quite clearly, is "love." God's second requirement is that something be loved. Before we get to what that something—*ḥesed*—really is, let us contemplate what "love" might be about. God wants us to love, which is not at all surprising, since God is love (1 John 4:8). How fascinating—and lovely: God "requires" (*daraśes*) love! God seeks love, God invites love, God enables love, God's heart breaks when there is a lack of love. God seems utterly uninterested in control. We may say that God is in control, but love by definition does not control. Love risks, love gives space to the beloved, love might not be loved in return. God seems rather unobsessed with adherence to rigid rules; God would not leave us cowering in fright. God loves; God's deepest dream is for us to love in return.

We could fill volumes talking about the meaning of love, and perhaps we should, since *love* is obviously a word that is flung around with reckless abandon. Love is a notion that has been degraded and abused. The most beautiful of all words, *love* gets glued on to all kinds of tawdry behaviors or glitzy pleasures. Yet our very awareness of the fact that love gets watered down and perverted proves we believe there is a real thing. Somehow, no matter what the pretenders, charlatans, and thieves of "love" do to twist love into something it is not, we know in the marrow of our soul that there is a real kind of love, a beautiful and true sort of love. We get glimpses of it here and there; our ultimate (if unacknowledged) life mission is to give and get such love, and we would literally abandon everything else we have or we fantasize about having for the chance at love.

Brilliant thinkers have written profoundly about love. C. S. Lewis gave a series of radio talks that became a great book, *The Four Loves*, in which he explored distinct Greek words used in the New Testament for love, from the erotic to friendship, from craving things to a deep, unconditional kind of love. Back in the late fourth century, St. Augustine probed two Latin words for love: *Uti* is the love of use; I love money or my job because it helps me get something else I really want. On the other hand, *frui* is what I really want; it is the love I simply love. He suggests we rather foolishly love God with *uti*, thinking we might use God to give a boost to our little projects. But God would be loved with *frui*: we love God simply because we love God and will do anything for God.

The Danish philosopher Søren Kierkegaard penned a wise book called *Works of Love* in which he leads the reader on a penetrating journey to discover that love is not merely about getting along or enjoying someone's company. Love is a duty, and only as a duty is love truly free. Love isn't what we feel only when we are loved in return; love simply loves. Love is about God: "To help another human being to love God is to love another man; to be helped by another human being to love God is to be loved."[1] After all, Jesus said, "You shall love." He wasn't predicting we would have strong feelings for somebody; he was commanding. Micah would say the Lord "requires" love.

In thinking of love as something that can be commanded, as something that involves work and a determined commitment, we are coming very close to the Hebrew word Micah used: *ahavat*. This word is used to describe what lovers feel for one another, but it also characterizes friendship and political allegiance. This *ahavat* kind of love is feeling, but so very much more. Hebrew "love" is loyalty, commitment, a dogged attachment; it is practical, evidenced by behaviors, actions, sacrifice, and habit.

So Micah urges us toward love, a significant, quite unflighty sort of love that isn't a mood but a way of life. But what is it that is to be loved in this case? The Revised Standard Version, used so frequently for two generations in Protestant churches, got us comfortable with the translation "to love kindness." We could certainly use some more kindness. We look around in our society and see an embarrassing rampage of rudeness, rage, and selfishness; *it's all about me, me, me, and you'd best get out of my way*. Television producers put on constant display the message that might makes right, so it is the biggest gun, the loudest shouter, the menacing, muscular presence that wins the day—and this kind of "force" finds its way into homes, offices, even churches. Simple kindness is underrated, and we can be sure God yearns for us to be kind.

But kindness is a mere sip from the delicious barrel that is *ḥesed*. Sharon Parks translated *ahavat ḥesed* as "to love tenderly."[2] Tender love pays attention to the capacity of the other person to be hurt and is aware that residing inside the other person's soul are lovely dreams. When Jacob is dying, it is *ḥesed* that Genesis 47:29 uses to describe his son Joseph's care for him; and the love between Abraham and Sarah, decades into their barren marriage, is called *ḥesed* (Gen. 20:13).

When we love with such love, we do so tenderly—but also tenaciously. It is this tenacity that tugs us closer to the heart of *ḥesed*. God wants tenacity to be loved, to be enacted, but it is a peculiar kind of tenacity—not an inner mood or determination, but a vital relationship, a commitment, a covenant. Many translate *ḥesed* as "covenant loyalty," and that is probably the best way to speak of what Micah says God wants us to love.

What could be meant by this "covenant loyalty"? Romantic novels, watercooler talk, Hollywood blockbusters, and even your psychotherapist will never, ever speak of "covenant loyalty." To understand *ḥesed* as "covenant loyalty," we have to travel back in time, to the Bronze Age. God miraculously rescued thousands of Hebrew slaves from the oppressive grip of Pharaoh—but why? Repeatedly Moses told Pharaoh, "Thus says the LORD, 'Let my people go, so they may worship me'" (Exod. 7:16; 8:16; 9:1; etc.). But the purpose of the exodus wasn't so the people could hold a little worship service with a song and a prayer. Worship for them was all of life; "covenant loyalty" is a firm commitment to the kind of thing Paul had in mind when he wrote, "Present your bodies as a living sacrifice, holy and acceptable to God, which is your spiritual worship. Do not be conformed to this world but be transformed . . . , that you may prove what is the will of God" (Rom. 12:1–2). The covenant between God and the people, prepared over many centuries, from creation through Noah's ark, from Abraham's faithful following through the crankiness of Jacob and his unruly sons, and finally unveiled through Moses on Mt. Sinai, is nothing less than the entirety of life being lived in intimate relationship with God. What is *ḥesed* but our heartfelt commitment to be the people of God, in liturgical worship but also in the worship of how we spend our free time or what we eat, how we herd our animals about, or farm, or pitch a tent, or make amends with someone we have hurt?

"Covenant loyalty," *ḥesed*, isn't something any one of us can (or wants to do) solo. We are not individual practitioners who in some isolated way love covenant loyalty. We are a people, a community, the nation of Israel, and then later the Church, the Body of Christ. We love *ḥesed* together; *ḥesed* is our compact with God and one another lived out in joy and faithfulness. The very first, primal definition William Holladay's *Concise Hebrew Lexicon* lists for *ḥesed* is "obligation to the community." The Brown-Driver-Briggs *Lexicon* notices *ḥesed* often means "doing favors for one another."

This we love. How intriguing that Micah did not say, "Do *ḥesed*," or "You'd better be loyal to the covenant or you are toast." Instead, we are invited to love *ḥesed*. In a way, the word *ḥesed* itself is a more profound kind of love than love itself. Tucked away inside this covenant loyalty is God's covenant loyalty, which is God's commitment to love, to be merciful, to stick with us in every obscure corner of our lives, through every conceivable circumstance.

In a way, the King James Version captured an important nuance of Micah 6:8 by translating "to love mercy." Mercy is a stranger to us, and yet mercy is the sorely missed stranger we hope will walk through our door one day. We are a permissive people; precisely because of that, we know no mercy. For there to be mercy, we must have a standard of goodness. A rowdy throng of voices in our society tells us to prove ourselves, to produce, to achieve our own worth; to fall short, to fail, is frowned upon, and you get left in the dust.

But don't we all crave mercy? Shakespeare called it "the gentle rain from heaven."[3] Jesus noticed how mercy is something we want to give and to receive: "Blessed are the merciful, for they shall receive mercy" (Matt. 5:7). Mercy never blames; mercy is bored by who deserves what. Mercy loves despite—well, it doesn't matter what comes after *despite*. Life's goodness is finally about nothing more or less than mercy given and received. George Eliot discerningly suggested that "when death, the great Reconciler, has come, it is never our tenderness that we repent of, but our severity."[4]

After all, a covenant is not a contract. In a contract, parties draw up a laundry list of conditions that, if unmet, invite severe consequences and a severing of the relationship. But a covenant is binding. In a covenant we have requirements, and yet we are stuck with one another; we have to work things out. The glory of *hesed* is the discovery that the way of love is entirely demanding, and simultaneously all mercy. In his analysis of *hesed*, Walter Brueggemann wisely says, "Our most serious relationships, including our relationship to the God of the gospel, are, at the same time, *profoundly unconditional* and *massively conditional*."[5] Because the Lord requires *hesed*, we deal with one another as our requiring Lord deals with us. In 2 Samuel 2:5, *hesed* is used to describe what David as a noble warrior does with his vanquished enemies: he is merciful and kind. No wonder Micah says to "love *hesed*." We would indeed love it if we experienced more mercy, if we gave more mercy.

So we never fear covenant loyalty, or dread it, or swallow it like medicine. We can love *hesed*. Our motivation around *hesed* isn't fear of infraction, but a deep desire, a constancy. We love love; we don't just fantasize about it or drudgingly enact it. We regard it fondly in the heart, and it dominates our thoughts; we celebrate its arrival and every good instance of *ḥesed* manifesting itself.

But the primary reason we can love *ḥesed* is this: God loves *ḥesed*. God thought it up! God actually *is* *ḥesed*. God revealed it to Moses—and God invites all of us into a relationship of *ḥesed*. So God must love *ḥesed* very much—so much that, from the Christian perspective, God sent God's very own Son on a mission that was the culmination, the sealing, the ultimate enactment of *ḥesed*. God most clearly loves *ḥesed*. Exodus 34:6 wonderfully declares that the Lord "abounds" in *ḥesed*; the loving covenant loyalty overflows out of God's own heart and immerses us in its flood. No wonder God wants *ḥesed* in return (Hos. 6:6); God "requires" it. But we blush when we realize we are surrounded with such beauty, and we would not dare reciprocate with anything less than our own love of this gracious, mind-boggling *ḥesed*.

So we then can love *ḥesed*. We can't really help ourselves, once we understand God's covenant loyalty, and the goodness and joy that issue from a life of covenant loyalty. We love that God fashioned us and the universe in such a way. We aren't alone; we aren't left to our own devices. Commitments have been made, and their inviolability is precisely what liberates us and settles us down so we can know peace, joy, and true pleasures at God's side.

To understand that loving covenant loyalty is not a legalistic checklist of merely doing the right thing, we might think of the musical *Fiddler on the Roof*. One day Tevye, the traditional Jewish papa struggling with a changing world and the marriages of his daughters, approaches his wife, Golda, and asks in song, "Do you love me?" Startled by such an inquiry, she responds quizzically, "Do I love you?" Then she protests: "For twenty-five years I've washed your clothes, cooked your meals, cleaned your house. . . . Why talk about love now?" Covenant loyalty asks, "Do you love me?" Yes, we've washed, cleaned, done one another countless favors, and have showered a steady stream of mercy on each other—and we love.

Perhaps *hesed* is the way a newlywed looks at the wedding ring and the promises made: being bound is freedom finally found; there is nothing I wouldn't promise or do for you. At Mt. Sinai, before the people had time to absorb the full content of the requirements Moses was bringing down, "the people answered with one voice, and said, 'All the words which the LORD has spoken we will do'" (Exod. 24:3). Once Jesus said, "Follow me," clueless fisherman simply dropped their nets and traipsed off to who knows where (Matt. 4:20). They would require much mercy, but they were forever caught up in the covenant loyalty of *hesed*, and nothing was ever the same.

8

TO WALK HUMBLY
WITH YOUR GOD

Finally we come to Micah's third requirement: to walk humbly with your God. The adverb "humbly" is rare in ancient Hebrew, so a few scholars have wondered what *hatznē'a* might connote. Hans Walter Wolff translates *hatznē'a* as "attentively," Delbert Hillers believes the best sense of *hatznē'a* is "wisely," and William Holladay's Lexicon suggests "carefully." [1] The only other occurrence of the root is in Proverbs 11:2: "When pride comes, then comes disgrace; but with the humble is wisdom." The antithesis of prideful arrogance is *hatznē'a*. And isn't it wise to be humble? Or is it that the humble are wise? And that wisdom is humility? If we are truly careful, aren't we humble? Isn't "humbly" the inner secret of "attentively"? If we are attentive to the truth of things, if we are attentive to ourselves and others in the light of God's mighty grandeur and tender compassion, aren't we led ineluctably to humility?

Micah 6:8 answers the question "With what shall I come before the LORD?" The answer, so simple yet so elusive, yet entirely possible and downright easy for us, is humility. Jesus told a parable about two men who went to the temple to pray: "The Pharisee stood and prayed thus with himself, 'God, I thank thee that I am not like other men. . . .' But the tax collector, standing far off, would not even lift up his eyes to heaven, but beat his breast, saying, 'God, be merciful to me a sinner!'" Jesus' favor was on the vile tax collector, for "every one who exalts himself will be humbled, but he who humbles himself will be exalted" (Luke 18:9–14).

The tragic humor in Jesus' story is that being humbled is unavoidable; so do we bow to the inevitability and the freedom of humility now? Or in our cocksure vanity have it come down on us unwelcomed? The world tells us to be strong, bold, and confident, but the posture of the people of God is articulated in the moving prayer of Psalm 131:

> O LORD, my heart is not lifted up,
>   my eyes are not raised too high;
> I do not occupy myself with things
>   too great and too marvelous for me.
> But I have calmed and quieted my soul,
>   like a child quieted at its mother's breast.
>   —vv. 1–2

We have been taught to be as titanic as possible, to strive to become more of a *have* and less of a *have-not*, to know the right people, to climb the ladder of success. No wonder upwardly mobile people are puzzled by God's Word, which constantly urges a downward mobility.

Jesus praises the people we would never hire or want to be like, since we think they will never amount to much: "Blessed are the meek, for they shall inherit the earth" (Matt. 5:5). Why did God choose Israel? "It was not because you were more in number than any other people that the LORD set his love upon you and chose you, for you were the fewest of all peoples" (Deut. 7:7). Didn't Samuel pass over the mighty older sons of Jesse before anointing little David, who in turn toppled the giant Goliath (1 Sam. 16–17)? Isn't faith really the same thing as humility? As Martin Luther put it, "Faith is the humility that turns its back on its own reason and strength."[2] Who was more humble, or had more faith, than Mary? When Paul admonished the first Christians, "Do not be conformed to this world but be transformed by the renewal of your mind," he targeted one type of conformity to avoid: "I bid every one among you not to think of himself more highly than he ought to think, but to think with sober judgment" (Rom. 12:2–3). But aren't we created in the image of God? Aren't we special? Yes! But our identity is a paradox. It is only when we realize our smallness, our relative insignificance, the brute fact that we are each not the center of the universe, that we discover our true greatness, our treasured place in the heart of God. Psalm 8 probably extols the hidden marvel of humility better than any other passage of Scripture:

> When I look at thy heavens, the work of thy
> fingers,
>   the moon and the stars which thou hast
>   established;
> what is man that thou art mindful of him,
>   and the son of man that thou dost care for
>   him?
> Yet thou hast made him little less than God,
>   and dost crown him with glory and honor.
>   —vv. 3–5

Only when in humility we can ask in dumbfounded wonder, "Who are we, so small, that you even notice us?" that we comprehend the true glory of the crown God has placed on our little heads. God became incarnate, not in the stalwart, muscular body of a tall warrior, but as a tiny, vulnerable infant: this is the glory of God, "holy infant, so tender and mild." Children understand, as they look up at grownups, smile, and sing:

> Jesus loves me, this I know,
> for the Bible tells me so.
> Little ones to him belong;
> they are weak, but he is strong.

Humility is not humiliation. God despises any time any of God's creatures are abused or ground into oblivion with words or violence; it is evil arrogance that dares to squash humble human beings God loves so much. We come before God, not strutting because we climbed on top of somebody else so God would notice us, but empty-handed and with humility.

What if we do well in the world and are applauded for our achievements? Thomas Merton offered a vivid image for us: "The humble man receives praise the way a clean window takes the light of the sun. The truer and more intense the light is, the less you see of the glass."[3] Humility shields us from ever thinking we have it all figured out. The humble can always receive direction; John Calvin spoke of the Spirit's wonderful gift of a "teachable spirit" (*docilitas* in Latin, whose English cognate is "docile").[4]

Of course, humility is tricky; the very effort to be humble can be the ruin of us. It was Lancelot du Lac in *Camelot* who boasted of his *humilité* when quizzed by Guinevere about the source of his prowess, and as the story unfolds we discover that the one who is proud of his humility suffers the most tumultuous fall, for his humility was nothing but the charade of the egomaniac. Humility is the simple truth about ourselves, but the truly humble glance away quickly, for their focus is not on their humility but on God. Perhaps it is only by a miraculous gift of the Holy Spirit that we can be humble in the manner Jesus alluded to when he spoke of the left hand not knowing what the right hand is doing (Matt. 6:3). Am I humble? I'm not really sure. I haven't noticed; I've been so focused on the Lord.

Micah 6:8 doesn't say, "Be humble," but "Walk humbly." In humility, we walk, we go, we are on the move. The Italian film director Pier Paolo Pasolini captured the mood of "walking humbly" in his 1964 film *The Gospel according to St. Matthew*. Whereas we may imagine Jesus sitting still, with disciples lounging around him and listening to his words, Pasolini depicted them as on the move: Jesus is walking all the time, and it's no pokey stroll; he's striding urgently. And he's constantly talking: looking back over his shoulder, teaching on the move. The disciples are nearly breathless, trying to keep up, trying to get his words while they are headed somewhere—now!

Walk humbly with your God. The humble are never passive; they do not shrink into the shadows and let the world pass them by. The humble are active, and more effectively so, since they don't get entangled in ego issues. Merton taught us that humility "is a virtue, not a neurosis. . . . Humility sets us free to do what is really good, by showing us our illusions and withdrawing our will from what was only an apparent good."[5] Before organizational Christianity was called "the Church," it was called "the Way." Where was Paul going when he was converted? He was headed to Damascus, to see "if he found any belonging to the Way" (Acts 9:2). With what will we come before the Lord? We begin by coming, by moving. What does the Lord require? That we walk, that we get going. We may fall down, but as the old saying goes, "If you fall on your face, at least you were moving forward."

But we do not simply walk, or even walk humbly. We walk humbly "with your God." God never waves good-bye and leaves us on our own out there. We walk *with God*, never alone. What was Jesus' last promise? "Go into all the world . . . and I will be *with* you always" (Matt. 28:19–20). At the very end of his long life, having traveled countless thousands of miles on foot or on horseback trying to bring the Gospel and a hopeful way of life to hordes of people, John Wesley uttered his last words: "The best of all is, God is with us."

And it is truly "us" that God is with when we walk humbly. Micah 6:8 doesn't say, "Walk humbly with God," but "Walk humbly with *your* God." God is yours? We don't need any encouragement to become possessive. God is God, and to think that I somehow possess God, that God is mine, is treacherous, even though I foolishly bumble into conceiving of God as a personal right of mine, tucked in my pocket to retrieve when needed.

Yet God is so merciful, God is so generous, God is entirely defined by self-giving that God lets God's own self become ours. God says, "Claim me as your own. You are mine, but miracle of miracles, I also am yours; we will not let any kind of distance come between us." The God who hurled the absurdly vast expanse of the universe into being, the God whose scope and power dwarf whole solar systems and galaxies, this God with whom we walk is personal and tender enough to let us speak of God as our own. This is why we can walk, and need not walk in any other way than humbly, for we walk with this stupendous God who is ours, and thus we are God's, and together we all walk for, and with, everybody else.

EPILOGUE

So there we have it. With what shall we come before the Lord? He has graciously shown us what is good. And what does the Lord require? What is it God seeks, provides, and delights in? The doing of *mishpat*, the love that is covenant loyalty, and the unspeakable pleasure in walking humbly with our God. Our imaginations are stretched and our hearts expanded by this threefold vision from the God who is three in one. On our own, we lunge toward justice, love, and humility, knowing we will fail, but the very desire to please God pleases God, and the Holy Spirit may just produce the fruit of Micah 6:8 in us. The world is even hungrier for it than we are.

APPENDIX: STUDY GUIDE

Kathy Wolf Reed

Tips for Leaders

When it comes to facilitating a meaningful group discussion, leader preparation is key. Before beginning your book study, make sure that you have read the text thoroughly, and decide how many sessions you will allow for discussion. The number of sessions outlined in this guide is merely a suggestion; if you find that your group has passion and energy for a particular subject, allow more or less time for certain chapters. For instance, if your group shows a particular interest in the authorship and historical context of the book of Micah, consider spending two sessions on chapters 1 ("Micah the Prophet") and 2 ("A Controversy"), and combine your study of chapters 6 ("To Do Justice") and 7 ("To Love Kindness").

As you introduce each session, give enough information so that someone who has not read the day's text will have a working understanding of the topic, but not so much information that participants have no motivation to prepare for the next session. The goal of this study is to engage participants in a way that is both enjoyable and meaningful.

Preparing Space

Prior to participants' arrival, ensure that the meeting space is conducive to discussion. Arrange chairs in such a manner that participants are facing one another (in a circle or gathered around a table). If you anticipate a large group, arrange chairs in several smaller groupings so that no group exceeds seven or eight members. As you arrange the room, prepare for participants who may have special needs, such as those with difficulty hearing or those who might appreciate being close to an exit.

Materials Needed

— Bibles
— Paper
— Pens
— Whiteboard or newsprint
— Markers
— Extra copies of this book

In addition to these basic supplies, some special research or materials are required for the optional activity that is part of each session. Be sure to read the instructions for these activities carefully, and take note of the special supplies that are required:

Session 1: copies of your congregation's weekly worship bulletin

Session 2: article from the week's news about someone "doing justice" in the world

Session 3: information about your congregation's or denomination's commitment to advocacy

Session 4: candle

Getting People to Talk

One of the greatest challenges of leading a group study can be getting participants to engage in discussion. If members of your group are accustomed to a lecture style of learning, it may be helpful to state clearly that this study is intended to be discussion based. Remind participants that in a discussion-based study, there are no right or wrong answers, but rather a wide variety of ideas and perspectives.

The discussion questions included in each session are designed to appeal to a variety of individuals. Some participants may jump into discussion with ideas they are excited to share. Others may need more time to process their thoughts. Here are a few techniques you may use to ensure that everyone has a chance to participate fully:

— When posing a question, ask participants to turn to a partner and discuss their responses before sharing them with the entire group.

— Do not be afraid of silence, and encourage others not to be as well. Some individuals need a few moments of quiet to fully articulate their ideas. Allow for this time by asking the group to take a few moments to think silently about the matter at hand. Then invite responses.

— Invite participants to build upon and/or challenge each other's ideas in a friendly, respectful manner. This technique is especially helpful when engaging quieter members: "How would you respond to [name]'s comment that . . . ?"

— If you find that you have participants whose thoughts and questions are straying a bit too far from the subject at hand, create a "parking lot" for these comments on a whiteboard or on newsprint. Record these questions and ideas in the parking lot, and have the group revisit them at the end.

SESSION 1

CHAPTERS 1 AND 2

Opening Prayer

God of the prophets,
we give you thanks today for the life of Micah,
who from tragedy found hope,
who in the face of injustice spoke your truth.
May his words be your word to us today.
In Christ's name, we pray. Amen.

Introduction to the Session

Participants will be asked to explore Howell's biographical illustration of the prophet Micah in chapter 1, as well as the controversial context from which Micah's words were first spoken, which is covered in chapter 2. These chapters lay the groundwork for a closer look at the Micah 6:8 text in the following sessions. Important to this particular discussion is the underlying question of why: Why, when there is so much that we don't know about the prophet Micah, is it important to explore his life and the circumstances under which he spoke?

Discussion Questions

1. Howell opens his book by saying, "We wish we knew more about Micah as a person" (p. 3). Ask participants, in partners or small groups, to create a list of what we do know about Micah based on the information found in chapters 1 and 2. Once partners have had a few moments to compile their list, have them share their responses with the group. Use these responses to come up with a master list titled, "Who is Micah?"

2. Howell states that "Micah was bold in denunciation, but he was even bolder in hope" (p. 5). Given what we do know about Micah, what do you think motivated his denunciation? What do you imagine motivated his hope?

3. As Howell speaks of Micah's use of legalistic language, he points out that "due legal process affirms the dignity of everyone involved" (p. 8). Ask participants to think of examples, biblical or contemporary, where human dignity was affirmed through legalistic processes. Can they think of examples when human dignity was

violated through these same processes? How do they understand God's justice to be similar or dissimilar to the human justice system?

Optional Activity

In chapter 2, Howell draws deeply on the image of a trial. Ask participants, in pairs or small groups, to look carefully at their congregation's weekly worship bulletin and see if they notice any elements that reflect this trial imagery. Is there a time of confession? Conviction? How are participants in worship "sentenced" with a call or charge? Returning to Howell's comment that legalistic language can be uncomfortable to believers, ask participants if they find this trial imagery unsettling or reassuring. Why?

Responding Question

Why is it important that we know this contextual information about Micah? How would our reading of Micah 6:8 differ if we learned that Micah came from a wealthy, prosperous family and held a position of great power in Jerusalem?

Closing

Let participants know which chapters you will be covering in your next session. (If you are following the suggested outline, this will be chapters 3, 4, and 5.) Ask them to pay particular attention to the idea of God's will for us, the various translations of the Hebrew *daraš*, and the relationship between God's justice, kindness, and humility.

If you plan to have your group participate in the optional activity in session 2, ask each member in the coming week to find a newspaper or online article about someone he or she sees "doing justice" in the world.

SESSION 2

CHAPTERS 3, 4, AND 5

Opening Prayer

Merciful God,
what you require of us is much,
and yet in life our greatest joy is found in serving
    you.
Help us to respond to your commands in love,
help us to seek justice, love kindness, and walk
    humbly
in all that we do
and with all that we are.
In the name of the Son, who lives and reigns
    with the Spirit,
one God, ruler of us all. Amen.

Introduction to the Session

In the second session, participants will use Howell's discussion of God's will in chapter 3 to consider how God reveals to us what is good here in our lives today. The idea of our response to God's goodness will then be discussed in terms of the Hebrew *daraš* ("require"). Finally, as Howell explores in chapter 5 the three things required of God's people, participants will discuss the inextricable relationship between justice, kindness, and humility.

Discussion Questions

1. In chapter 3, Howell states that "the whole witness of the Bible is precisely this: God has shown us what is good" (p. 12). Ask participants, in partners or small groups, to consider these questions: What are some examples of the goodness that God reveals to us (or through us) in our daily lives? Why do you think Howell says, "There remains a hidden dimension to this revelation of what God requires" (p. 14)?

2. In order to convey the full meaning of the Hebrew *daraš*, Howell offers several biblical references illustrating the verb's various uses. Have participants take a closer look at these passages (pp. 16–17) and consider the following question: Which of these verses—2 Samuel 11:3; Jeremiah 30:14; Deuteronomy 22:2; 1 Corinthians

13:5—do you think comes closest to capturing God's sentiments in Micah 6:8? Why?

3. Howell seems adamant that the command of God to practice justice, kindness, and humility is actually one requirement, not three. Ask participants to form three groups—one each for justice, kindness, and humility—and try to imagine how one might practice this requirement without the other two (for instance, practicing kindness without justice and humility). Is it possible? Why or why not? How is God's justice/kindness/humility distinct from a purely secular understanding of justice/kindness/humility?

Optional Activity

If you asked your group to gather news articles in the past week of people "doing justice" in the world, have them pair up and share their story with a partner. (If only some members of your group have a story to contribute, have these individuals pair with members who do not.) Ask participants to determine how or if justice, kindness, and humility are all demonstrated in the article they brought. Once they have had a few minutes to discuss, ask for partners to give a brief synopsis of their article to the larger group and tell how it relates to Howell's interpretation of justice, kindness, and humility in the book of Micah.

Responding Question

On page 20, Howell writes, "God doesn't require any *thing*; nothing external to ourselves will do. God requires us, ourselves, our lives, hearts, passion, zeal, devotion, time, thoughts, and love."

Thinking about their own commitment to the life of the church, ask members if they agree or disagree with Howell's statement. Is it not a requirement of Christian life to offer certain "things" (monetary gifts, gifts of food or clothing to the poor) to God and God's people? What does Howell mean when he says, "God doesn't require any *thing*"?

Closing

Let participants know that in session 3 you will be covering chapters 6 ("To Do Justice") and 7 ("To Love Kindness"), with particular attention to individual versus communal means of "doing justice" and to the meaning of the Hebrew words *mishpat* and *hesed*. If you plan on doing the optional activity in session 3 with your participants, ask them to spend some time at home looking for resources on how your congregation or denomination commits itself to advocacy for the poor and vulnerable.

SESSION 3

CHAPTERS 6 AND 7

Opening Prayer

Holy One, Holy Three,
have mercy upon us, an unjust people;
have mercy upon us, who so often turn away
    from kindness.
Help us to live into the calling to serve another;
help us to live into the calling to love one
    another;
give us communities of faith and strength
to hold us accountable when we need it most.
We pray in the name of the one whose selflessness
    is a gift and model to us all,
Jesus Christ. Amen.

Introduction to Session

In the third session, participants will look closely at Howell's interpretation of what it means to "do justice" within the context of a faith community, with particular attention to his understanding of the Hebrew term *mishpat*. The group will then look at how the Hebrew understanding of *ḥesed* influences the understanding of what it means to "love kindness" in the life of faith.

Discussion Questions

1. Howell notes that while the term "justice" may call to mind those who enforce laws for a living (lawyers, judges, etc.), through Micah's words, God was actually simultaneously speaking to each individual of the day and to the community of individuals as a whole. How is doing justice both a personal and communal commitment to God? What do individual acts of justice look like in practice? What do communal acts of justice look like in practice?

2. Through Howell's study, we learn that *mishpat* is one way of describing "God's dream for a special kind of community" (p. 31). He goes on to speak of the personal "rights" we enjoy in modern society. In partners or small groups, ask participants to create a list of rights that most people today would say are fundamental to communal existence. As a full group, share these lists and notice some of

the common responses. Then consider Howell's suggestion that in light of the Hebrew understanding of *mishpat*, "life is a *gift* of God; you do not have a right to a wage or basic necessities, since God has graciously created us as a part of a community where sharing and support are as natural as what a parent does for a toddler" (p. 32). What is your reaction to this statement? Does it strike you as inspirational or overly idealistic? Looking at your group's list of rights, is it possible that these individual rights can be detrimental to a community that embodies the true meaning of *mishpat*?

3. Howell remarks that "'covenant loyalty,' *hesed*, isn't something any one of us can (or wants to do) solo" (p. 44). Ask participants why it is that Howell seems to be putting such a heavy emphasis on the communal nature of responding to God's call. How is the idea of *hesed* as "obligation to the community" countercultural? Thinking of their own faith community, ask participants how *hesed* is demonstrated in daily life. Where do they see room for improvement in their personal practices of *hesed*?

Optional Activity

While most churches have some form of charitable commitment, less common is an intentional commitment to advocacy on behalf of the poor and vulnerable. Prior to the session, ask participants to do a little research on how your congregation or denomination engages specifically in advocacy. Ask individuals to bring information on local, national, or international organizations that are doing meaningful advocacy work and to share them with the group. What commitments does your faith community already have to advocacy? What possibilities do you see for further work in advocating for those who have little voice or power in society? Continue this activity with the following "responding question."

Responding Question

Howell says, "God's goodness is not to be hoarded, but spread around, made available for free to strangers" (p. 34). He clearly believes that when performing acts of justice, charity and advocacy cannot be separated. Ask participants to consider ways that their faith community spreads God's goodness. What concrete steps could they recommend to the leaders of your congregation?

Closing

Let participants know that in the fourth and final session of the discussion series, you will be covering chapter 8 and the epilogue. Ask them to pay particular attention to Howell's discussion of humility as well as his final charge to the reader.

SESSION 4

CHAPTER 8 AND EPILOGUE

Introduction to the Session

In this fourth and final session, participants will be asked to share their overall impressions of Howell's book, as well as look closely at what it means to be a humble but active follower of God in the world. The group will then discuss Howell's closing statement: "The world is even hungrier for [the fruit of Micah 6:8] than we are" (p. 57).

Discussion Questions

1. Before opening with a specific question about Howell's final chapter, ask participants to share their general impressions of the book. What

about this study did they find most compelling? Would they challenge or critique any of Howell's basic assumptions about the words of Micah?

2. Howell pays special attention to the idea that "the humble are never passive" (p. 54). Why is he careful to point this out? What are some mistaken assumptions we make in our culture about those who are humble? How might persons be both humble and bold in their practice of justice and kindness?

3. Howell ends his epilogue by saying, "The world is even hungrier for it than we are" (p. 57). To what specifically does "it" refer to? How are some ways that you see the world hungering for the justice, kindness, and humility discussed in this book?

Optional Activity

Invite your group to spend some time in intentional prayer about the topics you have discussed throughout the study. Light a candle, and begin to read the following quotes from Howell's book. Allow for stretches of silence (thirty to sixty seconds) in between the readings, and encourage participants to pray silently or aloud as they feel moved.

— "Who is like the Lord? . . . Micah was bold in denunciation, but he was even bolder in hope" (pp. 3 and 5).

— "God does not leave our waywardness unaddressed. . . . Due legal process affirms the dignity of everyone involved" (p. 8).

- "God has shown us in manifold ways what is good" (p. 13).
- "At the very point of receiving mind-boggling, unachievable mercy, our striving to do things for God and to offer up our very selves to God intensifies; we are then unbound and set free" (p. 21).
- "The one thing this one God requires happens to be three: 'to do justice, to love kindness, and to walk humbly with your God'" (p. 24).
- "The justice Micah 6:8 invites us to do is *mishpat*, sharing what God has given, enacting God's will not merely for oneself but for the people, and with a zealous determination to ensure . . . that even the most difficult, strange, hard-to-love person is loved and included" (p. 33).
- "'Covenant loyalty,' *hesed*, isn't something any one of us can (or wants to do) solo" (p. 44).
- "It is only when we realize our smallness, our relative insignificance, the brute fact that we are each not the center of the universe, that we discover our true greatness, our treasured place in the heart of God" (pp. 51–52).

Responding Question

Ask participants to return to their general impression of this book as begun with the first discussion question. To whom would they be most likely to recommend this study? Is there a certain demographic (age, economic, theological, or geographic) that would benefit from reading this book? Why? If they could sum up the charge or commission of this book in one phrase or sentence, what would it be?

Closing

End this final session in prayer, using either the method outlined in the optional activity, your own words, or the following words:

God of justice that knows no bounds,
of kindness that knows no end,
and humility that knows no pride,
stir within us the desire to know you deeply,
follow you fearlessly,
and live our lives as a prayer to you.
Amen.

NOTES

Chapter 1: Michah the Prophet

1. Hans Walter Wolff, *Micah: A Commentary*, trans. Gary Stansell (Minneapolis: Augsburg, 1990), 35.

Chapter 3: God Has Shown You What Is Good

1. *The Confessions of St. Augustine*, trans. Henry Chadwick (New York: Oxford University, 1998), 202.

Chapter 4: What the Lord Requires

1. John Calvin, "Commentaries on Joel, Amos, Obadiah, Jonah, Micah, Nahum," in *Calvin's Commentaries*, vol. 14, *Commentaries on the Twelve Minor Prophets*, trans. John Owen (Grand Rapids: Baker Book House, 1979), 337.

Chapter 6: To Do Justice

1. Walter Brueggemann, Sharon Parks, Thomas H. Groome, *To Act Justly, Love Tenderly, Walk Humbly: An Agenda for Ministers* (Eugene, OR: Wipf & Stock, 1997), 16.

2. Theodore W. Jennings, *Good News to the Poor: John Wesley's Evangelical Economics* (Nashville: Abingdon, 1990), 64.

3. Charles Dickens, *Bleak House* (New York: Signet Classic, 1964), 49.

Chapter 7: To Love Kindness

1. Søren Kierkegaard, *Works of Love: Some Christian Reflections in the Form of Discourses*, trans. Howard and Edna Hong (New York: Harper Torchbooks, 1962), 113.

2. Walter Brueggemann, Sharon Parks, and Thomas Groome, *To Act Justly, Love Tenderly, Walk Humbly: An Agenda for Ministers* (Eugene, OR: Wipf & Stock, 1997), 39.

3. William Shakespeare, *The Merchant of Venice*, act IV, scene 1.

4. George Eliot, *Adam Bede* (New York: Penguin, 1961), 62.

5. Walter Brueggemann, *The Covenanted Self: Explorations in Law and Covenant*, ed. Patrick D. Miller (Minneapolis: Fortress, 1999), 36.

Chapter 8: To Walk Humbly with Your God

1. Hans Walter Wolff, *Micah: A Commentary*, trans. Gary Stansell (Minneapolis: Augsburg, 1990), 181–82; Delbert R. Hillers, *Micah: A Commentary on the Book of the Prophet Micah*, Hermeneia (Philadelphia: Fortress, 1984), 76; William Lee Holladay, *A Concise Hebrew and Aramaic Lexicon of the Old Testament: Based upon the Lexical Work of Ludwig Koehler and Walter Baumgartner* (Grand Rapids: Eerdmans, 1972).

2. Quoted in Gerhard O. Forde, *On Being a*

Theologian of the Cross: Reflections on Luther's Heidelberg Disputation, 1518 (Grand Rapids: Eerdmans, 1997), 62.

3. Thomas Merton, *New Seeds of Contemplation* (New York: New Directions, 1961), 189.

4. John Calvin, *Commentary on the Book of Psalms*, trans. J. Anderson (Grand Rapids: Eerdmans, 1949), xl.

5. Thomas Merton, *Thoughts in Solitude* (New York: Noonday, 1956), 65.

CPSIA information can be obtained at www.ICGtesting.com
Printed in the USA
LVOW130111300812

296568LV00006B/1/P

9 780664 236946